still

ALSO BY ANAHITA JAMALI RAD

for love and autonomy

Published by Talonbooks

still

POEMS

ANAHITA JAMALI RAD

TALONBOOKS

Talonbooks
9259 Shaughnessy Street, Vancouver, British Columbia, Canada V6P 6R4
talonbooks.com

Talonbooks is located on xʷməθkʷəy̓əm, Sḵwx̱wú7mesh, and səl̓ilwətaʔɬ Lands.

First printing: 2021

Typeset in Garvis
Printed and bound in Canada on 100% post-consumer recycled paper

Interior design by Typesmith
Cover design by Anahita Jamali Rad

Talonbooks acknowledges the financial support of the Canada Council for the Arts, the Government of Canada through the Canada Book Fund, and the Province of British Columbia through the British Columbia Arts Council and the Book Publishing Tax Credit.

Library and Archives Canada Cataloguing in Publication

Title: Still : poems / Anahita Jamali Rad.
Names: Jamali Rad, Anahita, author.
Identifiers: Canadiana 2020036023X | ISBN 9781772012859 (softcover)
Classification: LCC PS8635.A3355 S75 2021 | DDC C811/.6—dc23

THIS PAGE IS INTENTIONALLY BLANK

FOLIATE PROCEDURES

a history is formed as
matter-filled time in its
poised selective memory

dis- + re-orienting particulars of
what's left, removed, or left removed

immediate, fragmentary, continuous
here or there, as impressions on skin
left dangling in the atmosphere

One therefore accepts the temporary mithridatic cost of revolutionary sacrifice (the immense discomfort of the one who waits and starves in jungles, deserts, or dark undergrounds), risking oneself before immediate trials of ascetic suffering and spent morality as an offering to the imminent collective, a reciprocal gift instructed by a terminology of the "I" forever becoming "we" and a transaction of the traded "this" for the pictured "beyond."

—Jason Bahbak Mohaghegh, *Insurgent, Poet, Mystic, Sectarian: The Four Masks of an Eastern Postmodernism* (2015)

LOG I

I waited for time to
reveal itself, for

skin extending to
mediate this sensed

pretending to experience
giving in to the

prodromal sinking or
collapsing to

functions of a subdermal
quiet that fills

when all your hope is
a foggy presupposed to

a purposeless wandering
or suppositions of how I

could climb a mountain
a thousand mountains

to get to my displaced
and contentless feeling for

even a memory of
idle inscription, yet here I

am now hidden in a
renunciation of

representational proximity obfuscated
by   the shape of my

sensorial appearances of labour-
time or of a feeling inside

a wavering of presence
that is

unacknowledged and unknown
still somehow designating

forms of my
wrenched and wretched

flung experience that
is, again, in fragments

LOG II

I waited for this
specific temporality

correlated the positioning of
my limbs to ground

to splinter a
priority of

a deferred commodity in
skin's removal that

used to drive me wild
still drives me wild

now this post-normative regret
is still scarcity

and only proximal to the
terminal possibilities of my

undialectical empty time that
is still a reliable tendency toward

can't get my
can't get my mind

still, in the absolute for you
where sentiment

of time repudiates
how I feel

a still, detached intensity
and maybe   I echo this air of

our dreamed future
our dreaded future

an asymmetry of time-experience performs
the intimacy between skin and a light breeze

still, to feel movement in
reveries of resource

when living in this livid
content scarcity and still

explicitly desiring an
authentic alternative to

an internal politic, a
detached propensity, or

alternative immediacy that's still
an enduring wishful feeling

everything is accompanied by its opposite
in this catastrophe as in any

we abandon
our errant experience

of historical discontinuity and
wishful transformative in/stability

a turn away from
what senses confirm

our self-reflexive banished is an
endless function of possible dazzling

diffraction standardizes enjoyment

of this felt
unavailable

institutionalized obsession is
in direct relation to

splitting time
built experience

when the givenness of time
necessarily mediates my

remote possibilities of
computational specifics

my prepositional transmission is
in real time

for when you get here
and I

LOG III

I waited every day
positioned it this way or that

my disjointed machinations felt
symmetrical to a potential in

exposing a persistence to find
new ways of dying for

those in unlevelled parts of space
and here I am, acting to get to

the heart of it
to our inmost possibilities

for a day like yesterday or tomorrow
when air just

stings a little
I lie without movement

my vision waves lightly
as if my head is a boat

as if this building is a
as if my to you

stuck in loops of these alienated trajectories
capital flows in waves, too

and maybe
this moment gradually becomes

something to look forward to
a felt configuration of

the sidewalk, the road, other buildings
carefully planted trees

new structures of language
of matter transposed

dislodged history or
vectors of colony

a pulsing in my head of
abnormal materialities

when rupture requires
life, take mine

obfuscation makes visible the
materials that constitute

the things that money mediates
and are peripheral to the

still immediate
still fragmentary

simultaneity of the past
still stuck in this loop

of where you and I

LOG IV

someone waited for this
it could have been me

in billowing sensations
a real-estate bubble gets fortified

thick determinacies move through
to transgress the space for

how I want my
dazzled para-aesthetic, finally

to mediate opacities of
still, occupied by space

where, in an increasingly hotter world
wealthy neighbourhoods with more greenery keep cool

husks of representation
mark the distance

and new green developments mean
fifty families go without housing

here, my severed is relative and these
mediated distinctions left me to

retract the falsely definitive
declarations of historical determinants

in difference, chasing the
yet still left to these precise devices

of markets operative to my weakened
metaphysical reflection

my thinly translucent perceptual shift in
skin that's ready to

can't touch the ready to
convulsive sometimes

my own is
ceaselessly mediated with

petty encroachments and
the reconciled   imaginary

workings of structures within
the indivisible elements

of our totality, our
opaque matter

to whose positional endings that
make me exhausted with my

non-historical traversing of
the negative

as if this space comes and
goes, *nothing is settled*

heterogenous filiation in
our discarded data is

vague-like, can't mean to
my undescriptive automatism

still, can't this
forced affective

fall in or out of
means nor ends

LOG V

I waited so this day could pass
as if time itself

could determine
action

days that passed before
pass again, unfolding

dimensions of imagining

and still I
position my position

peripheral to the object
as if I can

touch directly
in future shape

dissembled particulars that
organize immaterial time

make every flesh dispensable
in encounters and indeterminate durations

for when future
wants what it
wants

CONDITIONS OF SYSTEM-WIDE CRISIS

A STUDY OF THE MATERIALLY INCLINED

before the assumption that there is an end
there is boredom, suffering, and generalized pain

a textile covers
a crumpled garment on the bed
a lopsided shoe or teetering glass
papers strewn or folded neatly
people come and go, nature acts
real or unreal, time passes inadvertently

I keep the closets packed
undone organization
could go for a walk or not
no, probably not

movement is the enemy of stillness
I unvoice and unclaim language
refuse an active participation
do not make the slightest difference

shelves accumulate dust in
a layering of affective stimulus
I bathe only to forget the body

DAYS ARE MEASURED WITH THE PASSING OF LIGHT

several things occur simultaneously:
the sunlight hits the floor and a sliver of ankle

in a crisis, some prisoners are freed
while others are shot for attempting to escape

technical solutions are found for
making life and letting die

consumption is derailed
attention is distributed

profits from extraction of oil drop
while profits from extraction of personal data skyrocket

populations are kept alive
as a memory against uncertain futures

populations relate only in the virtual
a state of being that is not life, but may resemble it

non-linear time anomalies, a feedback relation or déjà vu
days are measured with the passing of light

everything is somehow still here materially
forms open and close

if I move slightly, my breath follows

IN THE EVENT OF A NEAR MISS

so I move around a little

I buy some time

I move around

but just a little

awash with
enacting

shaped
enjoyment
fear
grief
awe

this   *feeling* is
still parasitic

each of these objects
are still commodities

are seemingly necessary
are an active inactive

are as unlife or unliving

as this senseless scrawling

OVERFLOW POTENTIAL

Every system of violence starts with a word, a nightmare prescribed by a precision strike always in a state of war extraction, circulation, or a part-time revenge of the "I" that makes "you" and the "you" that makes "me" and somehow leaves no trace.

I only write to be unproductive. I only write of governmental neglect and war violence anxieties gone viral move the cursor and click into circulation. Despotic entrenchment slipped in codes an unruly mob or *finally* historical incivility forged in nondiscursive to this untamed morality.

Formed by the imperative to be an image displaced representation what you see and what you cannot see to internalize the desire to be ambiguous, a subject of democracy a free flow of free speech the fine line between a firm knock and a "even ghostly categories can be set against" the non-simultaneousness of the new.

Every new moment comes at the expense of other possibilities. Driven by an unrestrained vitalism this moment is a polyphonic dimension of circumstance here and now exhausted of residual outrage a participatory logic of dilating exposure keeps us in check.

Shifts in moments of a reversal of narrative, a breakdown of precision, affective publics unfold the unsafe and eroding of excess. A lost liberal ideal. Symbolic collapse of a critical void. A grilled cheese sandwich of aesthetics and politics. Release the valves. Force untranslatability.

Build structures of opacity.

Enact an array of leaking practices. Describe or prescribe an uprising. Radically displace symbolic borders. Submerge in materiality. Purportedly undo or violate the rigidity of structures. Erase the digital trace. Engage in theoretical frameworks. Spill an understanding of agency or collapse of subject/object relation. Unveil the possible. *Other information still needs critique.* Hack or unsettle. Slit open.

Make visible as language   the speed of sound or light   there and elsewhere   encountered within and without   with best intentions   in this, our emotive economy   to get the message through   in a decisive blow of unbound   injurious   speech builds on this multiplicity   not simply as itself, but both   as every sentence that comes out is   *rude* or *uncivil.*

NOTHING COUNTS AS AN ACT

IN / OUT

a breath comes in two parts
and sometimes I forget the first

say I disappeared, finally
I let my ghost wander the halls and streets of whatever wherever

the streets opened somehow
filled with the desperation of some life

when you're a ghost
you're empty all of the time

not enough alive for bare life
not enough alive for anything

NOTHING COUNTS

In the absence of human activity
light spreads over the city

a hidden presence or
negative action with
the aim of disappearing

a recessive potential that
appears only to disappear

A RETICENT ASSERTION

to forget is to obey

a containment or overflow of
what non-doing undoes

dissipates boundaries of
current structures

collapses chronology in
active predictabilities of

a stillness that moves
mountains in

microtemporalities of
the immediate present

some silence is violence

some silence frees desire from seeking ends
is minimal contentment

is both inside and outside a system

refuses itself

THIS LANDSCAPE IS PERSONAL

either the self is disembodied representation
or unrepresentable

technologies that touch, estrange
that map, make into capital
make every spectator into spectacle
constantly caress or bombard
extend and bloat the self
to produce and reproduce

this is an opening
an unravelling of structure

to turn from signal to noise
to make what's visible invisible
to remove the spectator
and the spectacle

*SLOW DEATH OCCUPIES THE TEMPORALITIES OF THE ENDEMIC**

* Lauren Berlant,
Cruel Optimism (2011)

UNCONCERNED COMPULSIONS

here, encounters have no content with which to counter the
world of drives and productivity

a gaze is not pointed, but is an interruption of linearity
punctuating this endless leisure of auto-exploitation

bodies transform into non-bodies
data points

exhausted with the dragging of their bones in
thickened air, in

this *worrying* situation

a potential for confrontation
when any action

entangled in the whims of capital

from here or there
individual or collective

could *provoke*
or is *ineffective*

THE BODY DISLODGED, THICK WITH NOTHING BUT PRESENCE

Experience destabilizes the body of objects, of deregulated shifts in motion, moves a new kind of economy. The body performs edges of space, ends ownership of the material, instead exchanges in behaviour.

The body aligns itself against the chair. The chair, sealed in space, borders here and there. Borders a definition by material or *let it be done*. In style, displayed like an arrangement to know, here or there, this or that, self or other, up or down, gathers worlds, a display of intimacy, directs a translation of body, purports to move, affects the edges of space, thickened by some stagnation, heavy. So heavy breath does not move.

The body forgets sometimes, too. How it used to breathe. How light it could be to breathe. How effortless. When air moved through the body, before its boundaries were so heavy, a density of materiality weathered by space, this unregulated destability.

WHEN HANDS MISHANDLE

The body disorients itself, free and open, finally, reaches out to the edges of the previously untouched. The body extends its limbs to the wall to catch itself, adds value to the wall. Here, the body reaches to touch the edges of what can be deemed profitable. The disoriented body builds a radically different technological age, decentres its points of departure. Throws the world up, intimately scales up and replaces by reputation systems. The disoriented body makes what was at once invisible to capital reappear, building markets out of the evasion of every barricade, the far reaches, the extremities that hold the structures of relation.

The disoriented body slips proximity, does not hold in place, threatens the alignment of space and relations. Is not simply directed toward a life worth living or a life that makes a living. Is topsy-turvy, not following direction, puts to use, builds an imaginary, finds a solution, fills the gaps, severs the relations, is only supplemental, does not deliver on promises, evades responsibility. And yet, is still within the bounds of capital.

WHEN THE BODY BECOMES NON-BODY

The disoriented body slips in and out of materiality, grips the left-behind, the slightly askew, the forgotten corners, is a non-body. The non-body has no centre from which to disrupt its systems, knows no boundaries, slithers across borders and over oceans, exploits all bodies and assigns hierarchical value systems in order to maintain its own legitimacy.

The non-body is everywhere. Material and immaterial, real or imaginary, shapes the world, finds new forms of extractive resources, exploits labour, shapes desires, analyzes behaviour, discriminates what life is valuable until no life is valuable. The non-body has no nervous system, no processing of the sensorial, *feels* nothing.

STILL, THE BODY

The body still seeks. The body does, however, consider how it can seek a place or a time that does not exist. The body considers how its militant materiality can reconcile its desire for that which is yet material.

The body is filled with anguish, bewildered. Still striving to make something that can move material to immaterial and immaterial to material, the body disengages from reality, disrupts speculation, and seeks only the present's foggy skies and closed horizons.

YOU MADE ME FORGET MYSELF I THOUGHT I WAS SOMEONE ELSE*

* Lou Reed, "Perfect Day," *Transformer* (1972)

MY LEAKING REPRESENTATION

I cracked the code somehow
of how to cease to exist
understood it just long enough to melt away

seep into the floorboards through
the cracks in the foundation
where the good earth has been hiding

I let the juice of my once-flesh rot there
drain to where the good dirt is still hiding
still waiting

to spread my thick and viscous-like once-flesh
over and through the porous dirt

it's quiet there for me
I can be restful there

and let gravity support this lumpy mess
this once-identity

I settle in the dirt waiting with
microbes splitting
cells in self-defence my
near-inert inching outwards
downwards and upwards on
this buoyant ground

my fading and varied is

conquered and alienated
bifurcated and altering

left behind every
identifying feature
each signifier of my being

I'm left fragile and disposable
with erasures made necessary

to disarticulate my
willing desertion

WITHOUT WARNING

An unbearable fullness of being in place is an unstable holding together, a soft resistance to participation in control, or an outlet to relation funnelled through relentlessly coded and circulated behaviour.

What counters distinctions of the consequence of staying still, not moving, or a passiveness of display, is the inevitability of emergent potentials, overfull with and welling into formation the indeterminacy of actualized futures.

Interdeterminacy hacked, movement halted, ubiquitous, non-linear, formative force is an irruptive impulsion stemming from overflow crisis, mass scale, active, and imperceptible.

For it is the great significance of all crises that they make manifest what has been hidden; they cast aside all that is relative, superficial, and trivial; they sweep away the political litter and reveal the real mainsprings of the *class struggle.*

—Vladimir Lenin, "Lessons of the Crisis" (1917)

ERUPTION

Eruption is the force by which the shifts of internal contradictions are measured. Eruption is the point at which being and non-being are resolved. A development is in motion: a movement of opposites.

DISRUPTION REORDERS

Disruption is passing or not. Disruption is exogenous and endemic, iterative and episodic, continuous and universal, self-organizing, self-actualizing, splits time, reorients space, is somehow full and empty, accidental and planned, *both* and *and*, *either* and *or*. Disruption is and is not staying still, forgetting consumption, limiting the scope.

Disruption alters without warning.

RUPTURE

Rupture is seeing both sides. Rupture is movement by staying still. Rupture is the point at which *other* is subsumed into the understanding of *self*. The universalizing of capital turned the individualizing of late capital, or when opposites transform into one another. Concrete forms are assumed. The fabric of identity is altered.

*VISIBILITY WAS A TRAP**

* Wendy Hui Kyong Chun, *Control and Freedom: Power and Paranoia in the Age of Fiber Optics* (2005)

NEW CODES OF EXPOSURE

tangled in a self-automating
heap and left with

gesticulations of identity, a ghostly
signification of non-knowledge

either we desired it or
remembered forgetfully

our willed abandonment
of where we stand

the lines we draw
the places we belong

with waking eyes
splintering strangulation

and unburdened by
our subjective experience

our unburdening refrain
a delirium, in a sense

when there's nothing left
in this, our abandon

our inward-
looking silence

clears nothing
and is simply

a hesitant wandering
a tiredness of talking or
unwillingness to speak

this word-filled space seeks
its own absence

unwaking eyes that
exhaust the possible, unform

angulated and mangled
formless anxiety

this always-disaster is my
designed destitution, my
forever regret of being

fractured and
choosing erasure

vanishing exile in a
discrete recurring

my enclosed memory
is still

causal

... with no acceptable narrative to rely on, with no sustained permission to narrate, you feel crowded out and silenced.

—Edward Said, *Culture and Imperialism* (1993)

THE MATERIAL CONSEQUENCES OF DETERMINING MEANING

kept it to the point
our readiness
to assist

our willingness
to cooperate

we feigned innocence

our civil society is
impudent forgetting

feeble abandon
discrete slipped-into
never wanted to consider

this scorched disappearance that
names this wandering
to forget

A MECHANISM FOR NEW KNOWLEDGE

I was there
on the other side of circulation

practising sadness
stillness amid ruin

doing nothing in a
wakeful sorrow

my unmoving behaviour is a
surplus paralysis

they tried to move me
but I was unmoved

I kept it under lock
my true feelings

my implicated dismantling
a sort of meaning-making

preoccupied with that which
is hidden, *I let it all pass by*

an expert at non-being
I oscillate, burn the object

at the point of becoming, I
quiver, fluctuate, tremble, pulsate, flutter

I draw a cypress tree
under which I purport to dream

not figment
or movement

not speaking words or reaching a
textual untelling

I draw a cypress tree
under which I purport

an inexistent consciousness
an unknowing indecipherability

a cunning contention that is
well-prepared barbarism

perpetual and devastating
toward or away from the vocal

illegible or illegal

these compressed mechanisms
of imprint

to dispossess of identity
and forget difference

an even madness of
past and place

undoing the knots that   hold
to trace   future recollection

risking, daring
extant dimensions

and still, stripped of experience
would never presume to experience

THE PAGE FINALLY DISAPPEARED

A FINAL EMPTY-HANDEDNESS

memory formed / unformed
degenerates to generate

historically lived
inflated ideologies
ritualistic formations

["dispossessing both the ancestor and the descendant"]*

my aversion enabled
it to speak

to recontextualize my object
to recontextualize my

I structure my desire
for desire

through movements forged
of former worlds

* Jason Bahbak Mohaghegh,
Silence in Middle Eastern and Western Thought: The Radical Unspoken (2013)

moving without words
moving without hands
moving without

my inactive disposition
my unyielding incoherence

forms a means to
yet still

structured by
my desire to
emulate the commodity

automate non-knowledge
formed but never
acted

my aversion to be
subject

still forms this
congested subjectivity

still this mimetic
non-compliancy, still
dismantling uncertainty

this eruptive
tautological desire
for non-being's
silencing of language

requires a further frenzy
an empty volatility

[of movements forged of other worlds
of movements forged of future worlds

A DISTORTED AND DEEP PARALYSIS

we looked elsewhere
silently becoming
recur our fracturing

still displacing this
exhausted disaster

saturating our perception of
unending calamity

these cacographic
endotic procedures

distort multiplicity
this voiceless vertiginous insomnia

shaken by my unsaid
refusing performativity
by rival movement

of this shapeless
transfiguration of experience

of this untold desire

or an imprisoned abandon
still expecting
recollection

an eternally wrenched motion
an unbound wandering that is

conflated, mangled
extractive, defies continuity

exhausted of the words
I make of myself

    in this map of

        absent space

once suffocating my
depleted becoming

my left-behind identity
that still defi(n)es

in that it is still
encountered in inscription

EXCESS EXHAUSTS THE GIVEN

quietly I sit in
any / every given moment

in this unregulated
material ground

against my own repercussions
an idleness that proposes gesture

a self-suffocating
inside / outside

this silence is
no accident

diluted and
blurred or blurring

where memory-objects
de / generate between

gaps made material
a disruptive non-doing

THE FORMLESS PRECEEDS THE FORM*

this third-world text is
a ghostly society
a disregarded unreality

is a future or abyss
looming or impersonal

is of intimate partitions and
unconcerned compulsions

an inconsolable interiority to an
inconceivable outside

* Jason Bahbak Mohaghegh,
Insurgent, Poet, Mystic,
Sectarian (2015)

this text has no centre
no expectant crowd
no collective experience

freed from doubt
this text is unburdened by time
eliminates itself from both being and non-being

this text wastes matter
unforms the incommunicable

leaves nothing
to be asked or answered

this text is
subjective amusement
represents nothing

interrupts exteriority
is a fractal unreal

drapes untruth
and reads itself

into unfinished

STILL

straining a dissolution
an absent shiver
looking without
seeing

and *maybe I disappeared,* finally
without knowing
what parts of me belong where
or anywhere

I made myself irrecoverable
like dissipating smoke
an indication of what once was

since, finally, *I disappeared*
without material or history
without a body
or a place to be buried

THIS SILENCE IS NO ACCIDENT

this immediate and momentary sensation of skin on woven
wool upholstering this structure that holds my packaged
flesh that somehow relates me to gravity

is an absence of everything else

this simple pleasure of being still
becomes nothing, too

becomes a distorted paralysis
my motionless body shifts

perspective, too, this
silent body estranges

slouches in the negative
space of accumulation

dispossesses and
collapses itself into

pauses

waves in
vacuous disquiet

this sanguine play-acting of being in the world is a
disillusioned giving-in to

what massacre still waits

this bloodied sentence
is not even a sentence

to write:
I want the body to disappear

and then forget about it

roads turn to dust
and this
attention shifts by olfactory
and this
half-assed attempt at memory
can never really

EVERYTHING MOVED QUICKLY SO I SLOWED DOWN

without a hand to feed out of
this whole body
is divided

a rock or stone, too, transforms
is moved to shape
is weathered to future
is history transcribed

and my carved enthusiasm marked in future form is
a restless inaction, still
a wait-and-see strategy

for what part of
I can do nothing
yields paralysis

or hands held too close to touch

IN SLOW

horizons of heavy grey mist
mute every point of escape

even optimism of a future memory
of the smell of fresh leaves
is flattened

the road bends the asphalt
like splintering ceramics under
the weight of weather

SUCH ANGUISH

even now
I can taste it
my future sad self
in lost action
failed relation
weathered history

kept for future study
a remnant of geology

failed movement

stayed low close to the ground
kept the dirt in my fingernails
learned nothing
abandoned my desires
until there was nothing left of them

felt no regret
and had nothing to show for it

in any historical moment
an opening in the present is only imagined
half-forgotten

Anything that is not reified, cannot be counted and measured, ceases to exist.

—Theodor W. Adorno, *Minima Moralia: Reflections from Damaged Life* (1951)

I DISAPPEARED

I stayed, still
waiting

for the right external conditions
for my internal contradictions to

shift my
being to *non-being*

shift my
self to *other*

IN THE DEAD OF NIGHT

say I disappeared, I died
buried whole, or in pieces, who cares
I ceased to exist, it's over, done with

I put an end to this solipsistic individuality that
exists only in a capitalist nightmare
exists only in abstractions of the subject

exists only when equivalencies are made
between the time it takes to make a thing
and how much someone will pay for it

or when nourishment sold to one body
is valued at the life of another

and when some bodies stand up to it
driven by this so-called death wish of
no future for some future and lose
their bodies, no one even notices

say, burn the streets
the roads, the sidewalks
break the bank, really break it

then say, I disappeared
I fucking died, who cares
I was only there to fill the coffers of the rich, anyway

kill the "I"
rewrite history
burn all flags
burn all bridges, burn
personalized programs
facial recognition software
free delivery

and invent a new language

*invent new souls**

* Edward Said,
Culture and Imperialism (1993)

Life is therefore also a contradiction which is present in things and processes themselves, and which constantly originates and resolves itself; and as soon as the contradiction ceases, life, too, comes to an end, and death steps in.

—Mao Zedong, *On Contradiction* (1937)

ACKNOWLEDGMENTS

For their help with this project, I would like to thank S F Ho, Jeff Derksen, Nasrin Himada, David Bradford, Catriona Strang, and Claire Lyke. This work began at the Feminist Art Collective residency in the company of Lauren Brown, Michaela Bridgemohan, and Regan Henley. Some of these poems were written at the Tasarım Bakkalı residency organized by Yunus Emre Akçora and Işıl Şipal.

These poems were written with the support of the Canada Council for the Arts.

Anahita Jamali Rad is a text-forward artist born in Iran and currently based in Tiohtià:ke on the Traditional Territory of the Kanien'kehá:ka. Informed by anti-imperialist materialist theory, Jamali Rad has exhibited and performed across Canada and the United States, as well as in the United Kingdom and Turkey. They co-run House House Press with David Bradford.

anahitajamalirad.com